Speaking of families, how's your dad?

Still having a hard time adjusting. He called a few minutes ago.

I guess his call irritated me.

Well, chill. Life's a beach, y'know!

Oh, I just stopped to get a smoothie.

Give her a chance, Char. She might be nice.

There she is!

Hi.

How was your flight?

Good.

Same stupid question every year.

And your mother?

Good.

Like you care.

Hello?

For Heaven's sake, Pooja! Say hello to Sanjeev!

...

POOJA!!!!

BWA-HAH-HAH!

Um, I...uh... Well...

What **are** they doing out there?

You--you have a pet dolphin?

She's no pet!

She's my good luck mascot!

It was four, maybe five years ago, right along this beach...

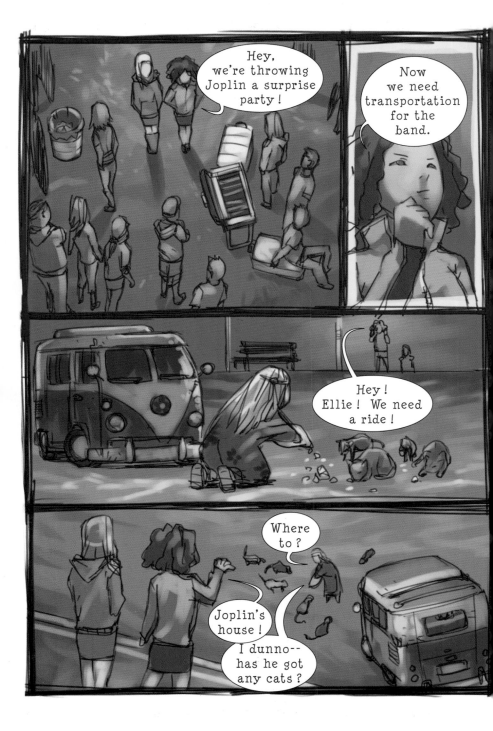

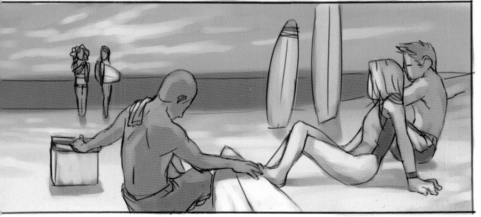

It's that fancy board. You could do it on this one.

Yeah? Maybe you could show me how.

Maybe I could.

Okay. Pop up.

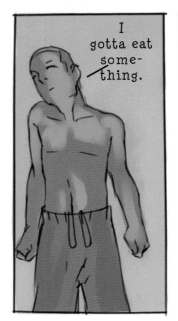

I gotta eat something.

I'm hungry too, but I'm not going home.

You think **I'm** going to eat with Randi Smiley Face?

I hate eating in that empty house.

I already have my first student.

Danny from the bakery asked if I knew an instructor!

...And now she does.

I think you'll be a great teacher!

There's your second student, Kahuna.

What do I charge?

My dad'll know. He's the marketing expert!

Sure! Ask him what to charge for lessons!

May I have Suki's hand in marriage?

Whoa!

Where'd that come from ?!?!?

Ooops! Sorry!

WATCH IT!!!

Nice **BAD**itude.

Nice everything.

It starts with an INNOCENT QUESTION...

Wuzzup, Tim? Didn't you like the movie?

...that leads to a CHALLENGE...

Like you could do better!

As a matter of fact, I could!

Prove it!

...that becomes an OBSESSION...

Well, I do have a video set-up...

Video ?!?!? You mean like a movie?

But my way--

I don't care! This is my movie-- remember?

...and finally EXPLODES in ANGER!

Aw, forget it! I QUIT! Do what you want!

It's

LIFE !
CAMERA !
ACTION !

starring

Serenity !

While "Life !" goes on everybody's favorite
blue-haired oddball and her friends turn their
energy and talents behind the "Camera !" to make
"Action !" movies with a decidedly different perspective !

Coming Soon from Thomas Nelson and Realbuzz Studios -
four BRAND NEW Serenity stories !

Serenity Vol. 7

Space Cadet vs. Drama Queen

Serenity Vol. 8

Sunday Best

Serenity Vol. 9

Choosing Change

Serenity Vol. 10

Girl Overboard

...and
featuring
these
"movies" !

For more info visit
www.SerenityBuzz.com
www.RealbuzzStudios.com

TERROR FROM THE TARANTULA NEBULA
Deep space voyagers discover a sinister secret!

CRAWLING FROM THE WRECKAGE
All exits blocked! Earthquake at the mall!

ESTHER, QUEEN OF PERSIA
A Biblical epic of romance and intrigue!

FRAULEIN STEIN'S MONSTER
Monster mayhem marks a remarkable revelation!